THI̲̲̲̲ ̲̲̲̲.̲̲̲̲

̲̲̲̲̲̲̲̲̲̲̲̲̲̲̲̲̲'S

JOURNAL

DATE : ̲̲̲̲̲̲̲̲̲̲̲̲̲

EAT THIS JOURNAL

A NOTEBOOK FOR FOOD LOVERS

CREATED BY STACY MICHELSON

RP STUDIO

PHILADELPHIA

RP Studio™
Hachette Book Group
1290 Avenue of the Americas,
New York, NY 10104
www.runningpress.com
@Running_Press

Printed in Singapore
First Edition: June 2021

Published by RP Studio, an imprint of Perseus Books, LLC,
a subsidiary of Hachette Book Group, Inc. The RP Studio
name and logo is a trademark of the Hachette Book Group.

ISBNs: 978-0-7624-9805-5

COS

10 9 8 7 6 5 4 3 2 1

RECIPES TO TRY

DON'T FORGET TO WRITE DOWN WHERE YOU GOT IT!

Grocery list

SALT ISN'T SCARY!
BE CONFIDENT
JUST USE YOUR HAND. THROW AWAY YOUR SALT SHAKER
ALL SALT IS FROM THE SEA!
SALT IS A MINERAL: SODIUM CHLORIDE
WE CANNOT SURVIVE W/OUT IT
ITS PRIMARY ROLE IS TO AMPLIFY FLAVOR!
FOOD SHOULDN'T TASTE SALTY, YOU SHOULD JUST TASTE THE INGREDIENTS BETTER!
SEASON FOOD WHILE COOKING, NOT AT THE END, NOT W/ A SALT SHAKER
10–12 INCHES
SALT AT A HEIGHT!
DISTANCE = SALT SPREAD EVENLY + EFFICIENTLY
KOSHER
• TEXTURE + FLAVOR
• JAGGED, ROUGH SHAPE STICKS TO FOOD
• MORE CONTROL TO GRAB + RELEASE
• EVERYDAY COOKING
SEA SALT
• FINE OR MEDIUM CRYSTALS
• GOOD FOR EVERYDAY COOKING, SUCH AS POTS OF H2O, ROASTS, TOSSED W/ VEGGIES, IN DOUGHS OR BATTERS
JUST AVOID IODIZED TABLE SALT. IT'S HEAVILY PROCESSED, BLEACHED + OFTEN HAS ANTI-CAKING INGREDIENTS ADDED TO IT.
SALT
MALDON OR FLEUR DE SEL
• SPECIAL SALT
• USE FOR TEXTURE
• GARNISH COOKIES OR CARAMEL
FLAT FOOD = UNDERSALTED FOOD

RECIPES TO TRY

DON'T FORGET TO WRITE DOWN WHERE YOU GOT IT!

Grocery list

LD BREW IS A BREWING
THOD, NOT A STYLE OF
VING COFFEE, BUT IT MOSTLY
EARS ON MENUS AS AN
D COFFEE DRINK. COLD
W IS A WAY TO SAY
D-BREWED COFFEE, AS
OSED TO TRADITIONAL COFFEE
T IS MADE W/ HOT H₂O.
A CONCENTRATE YOU CAN
K IT W/ BOILING H₂O TO
KE A HOT CUP OF COFFEE
POUR IT OVER ICE

MAKE IT AT HOME + GET CAFFEINATED FOR WAY LESS MONEY

1. START w/ COARSELY GROUND COFFEE, 1 CUP FOR 32 OZ OF H_2O IS GOOD
2. COMBINE IN A LARGE JAR, PITCHER, FRENCH PRESS, OR BOTTLE + STIR
3. LEAVE IT ON THE COUNTER FOR 12 HOURS OR STICK IT IN THE FRIDGE FOR 24, UP TO YOU!
4. STRAIN IT + STORE IN FRIDGE

W IT'S MADE

- BREWING COFFEE
TIME INSTEAD OF
T TO MAKE COFFEE.
RSE COFFEE GROUNDS +
M TEMPERATURE OR COLD
ARE COMBINED + LEFT
IT FOR 12-24 HOURS,
ATING A
NG +
CIOUS
W

ET
IRD
BRANDS
OTHER
EDIENTS
HE MIX,
SUGAR,
AMON,
LLA,
T, CITRUS, OR
TED CHICORY. IF YOU'RE
ING YOUR OWN, WHY NOT
RIMENT? YOU CAN ALSO
COLD BREW IN COCKTAILS,
KES, FLOATS + MORE!

L ICED COFFEE
OT COLD BREW!

COFFEE
H_2O
TIME
+ STRAINER
THIS STUFF!

COLD BREW

THE FLAVOR IS SMOOTH + DELICATE, LESS ACIDIC + LESS BITTER THAN THE REGULAR STUFF. IT HAS MORE CAFFEINE + IT'S EVEN EASIER ON YOUR STOMACH

ORIGIN

IT'S BEEN POPULAR IN KYOTO, JAPAN SINCE THE 1600s. LEGEND HAS IT THAT DUTCH TRADERS SHOWED THEM HOW TO BREW COFFEE W/OUT FIRE. KYOTO-STYLE COFFEE IS MADE BY DRIPPING H_2O ONE DROP AT A TIME OVER GROUND COFFEE, TAKING ANYWHERE FROM 5-12 HOURS

BUY IT PREMADE IN BOTTLES, BOXES, CANS + CONCENTRATES

YOU DON'T NEED ANYTHING FANCY TO MAKE IT, BUT THEY DO SELL COOL BREWERS, BOTTLES + BAGS TO MAKE IT EVEN EASIER

RECIPES TO TRY

DON'T FORGET TO WRITE DOWN WHERE YOU GOT IT!

Grocery list

CHILES

"HILE", "CHILI", OR "HILLI" ... YOU'LL SEE [IT] SPELLED DIFFERENTLY [D]EPENDING ON WHERE [YO]U ARE IN THE WORLD, [B]UT "CHILE" IS [CO]NSIDERED THE CORRECT [W]AY. IT'S BOTH THE SPANISH [SP]ELLING + PRONUNCIATION [TH]AT CAME OUT OF MEXICO

JALAPEÑO
- EAT RAW, PICKLED, COOKED, OR STUFFED
- POPULAR IN TEX-MEX, MEXICAN, AMERICAN STADIUM + BALLPARK FOOD
- SHU = 2.5k - 10k

CAYENNE
- MOSTLY USED AS A GROUND SPICE, BUT POPULAR USED FRESH IN STIR-FRY DISHES + IN SOUTHEAST ASIAN CUISINE
- SHU = 30k - 50k

POBLANO
- USE FOR CHILES RELLENOS, FLAVOR SAUCES + SOUPS
- MILDLY SPICY, EARTHY + BRIGHT
- SHU = 1k - 2k

HABANERO
- AROMATIC + INTENSE
- GREAT RAW, COOKED, PICKLED OR IN HOT SAUCE
- SHU = 100k - 350k

SERRANO
- LONG, SKINNY + BRIGHT GREEN
- EAT 'EM RAW, COOKED, ROASTED, SMOKED, OR IN TEQUILA COCKTAILS!
- SHU = 10k - 25k

SCOVILLE SCALE
INVENTED IN 1912 BY WILBUR SCOVILLE, IT'S USED TO MEASURE SPICINESS BY DETERMINING CAPSAICIN CONTENT—THE HEAT! SHU = SCOVILLE HEAT UNITS

A CHILE'S HEAT IS IN ITS VEINS + SEED POD, NOT THE SEEDS THEMSELVES

CHIPOTLE
- SWEET, SMOKY FLAVOR W/A SUBTLE HEAT
- USE IN SALSAS, SOUPS, STEWS + SAUCES
- SHU = 5k - 10k

THE **BIGGER**, THE [B]LANDER, THE **SMALLER**, THE SPICIER!

THAI / BIRD'S EYE
- ESSENTIAL IN THAI + SOUTHEAST ASIAN CUISINE!
- TINY, BUT POWERFUL
- SHU = 50k - 100k

SHISHITO
- WRINKLY + THIN
- MILD FLAVOR, BUT, 1 IN 10 CHILES IS <u>HOT</u>!
- SHU = 100 - 1k

RECIPES TO TRY

DON'T FORGET TO WRITE DOWN WHERE YOU GOT IT!

Grocery list

NATIVE TO THE AMERICAS, AVOCADOS HAVE BEEN EATEN BY PEOPLE IN MEXICO + CENTRAL AMERICA FOR MORE THAN 10,000 YEARS

THE NICKNAME "ALLIGATOR PEARS" NEVER REALLY CAUGHT ON

AVOCADO TOAST

ALTHOUGH AVO SANDWICHES ARE A VERY HIPPIE, 70s, CALIFORNIA VEGETARIAN THING — IT WASN'T UNTIL THE 90s THAT AVO TOAST STARTED SHOWING UP ON MENUS IN AUSTRALIA, A DECADE BEFORE IT DID IN THE STATES

AVOCADOS FROM CALIFORNIA

THE HASS AVOCADO WAS A NEW VARIANT OF A TREE THAT POSTAL WORKER RUDOLPH HASS STARTED GROWING IN LA HABRA, CA. HE PATENTED THE AVO IN 1935 + IT SOON BECAME THE MOST POPULAR VARIETY TO GROW + SELL, KNOCKING OUT THE FUERTE AVOCADO. HASS HAD THICKER, BUBBLY SKIN, SO IT HELD UP BETTER IN SHIPPING, CREAMIER FLESH + A LONGER GROWING SEASON. RUDOLPH'S TREE BECAME THE MOTHER TREE + ALMOST EVERY HASS TREE IN THE WORLD CAN BE TRACED TO HIS TREE. IT LAUNCHED MILLIONS OF TREES BEFORE IT DIED IN 2002

YOU'RE NOT ADDING SALT TO YOUR AVO, YOU'RE NOT LETTING IT REACH ITS FULL POTENTIAL! IT AMPLIFIES THE FLAVOR

AVOS HAD A HARD TIME IN THE 80s — THEY WERE SEEN AS A FATTY FOOD. THEN IN 2000 THEY BECAME A SUPERFOOD!

HIGH PRICES

PRICES HAVE SKYROCKETED 129% IN THE LAST FEW YEARS, DUE TO FACTORS SUCH AS LABOR, H_2O + CRIME. IT'S EXPENSIVE TO GROW, PICK, PACK + DISTRIBUTE THEM TO EVERYONE WHO WANTS 'EM. AVOS ALSO NEED LOTS OF H_2O + THE DROUGHT + HEAT WAVES HAVE HAD DEVASTATING EFFECTS ON THE INDUSTRY. THE POPULARITY + HIGH PRICES HAVE ALSO ATTRACTED CRIMINALS IN MEXICO TO EXTORT FARMERS

RECIPES TO TRY

DON'T FORGET TO WRITE DOWN WHERE YOU GOT IT!

Grocery list

RANCH

RIGINAL RECIPE
BUTTERMILK, MAYONNAISE, OUR CREAM, DRIED PARSLEY, DRIED ONION, DRIED GARLIC

ANCHERS IN TEXAS AVE BEEN MAKING UTTERMILK-BASED ALAD DRESSING INCE 1937

COOL RANCH DORITOS HIT TORES IN 1987!

PRETTY COOL

YUM!

AMERICANS LOVE TO DIP + POUR IT ON **EVERYTHING:** PIZZA, FRENCH FRIES, BUFFALO WINGS, CHICKEN FINGERS, CHIPS, BROCCOLI, CARROTS, CELERY, FRIED ZUCCHINI, BURGERS + WRAPS!

FAT & YUMMY

CANCELS OUT SALADS

AMERICA'S #1 DRESSING SINCE 1992

Made Them Rich.

SO SO RICH!

IT'S CALLED RANCH DRESSING BECAUSE IT WAS **CREATED ON A RANCH!** STEVE + GAYLE HENSON BOUGHT A DUDE RANCH IN SANTA BARBARA, CALIFORNIA IN 1954, WHICH THEY NAMED HIDDEN VALLEY RANCH! THEY SERVED THEIR SALAD DRESSING TO GUESTS + **IT WAS INSTANTLY POPULAR!**

GUESTS COULDN'T GET ENOUGH, SO THE HENSONS STARTED A MAIL-ORDER BUSINESS, SELLING PACKETS OF THE HERBS, WHICH WERE TO BE MIXED W/ BUTTERMILK + MAYO AT HOME

1973 THE CLOROX COMPANY BOUGHT THE RECIPE + NAME FOR **8 MILLION BUCKS**

1980s – RANCH STARTED APPEARING **AS A DIP!**

1983 – A SHELF-STABLE BOTTLE OF HIDDEN VALLEY RANCH LANDED IN STORES

1990s – IT BECAME A FAST FOOD CRAZE + WAS ADDED TO JUNK FOOD

RECIPES TO TRY

DON'T FORGET TO WRITE DOWN WHERE YOU GOT IT!

Grocery list

MUSHROOMS

BUTTON
- ST COMMON
- LLOW, EARTHY
- A WHITE
  SHROOM

MOREL
- AVAILABLE IN THE SPRING
- PICKED WILD
- NOT FARMED
- EARTHY, WOODSY, NUTTY
- EXPENSIVE

CHANTERELLE
- GOLDEN COLOR
- FRUITY, PEPPERY
- GREAT W/ PASTA, BUTTER

AVOID SLIMY, DAMP SHROOMS 2) STORE IN A PAPER BAG IN FRIDGE 3) CLEAN W/ A DAMP TOWEL

ENOKI
- LONG STEMS, SMALL CAPS
- POPULAR IN ASIAN COOKING
- GREAT IN SOUP

PORTOBELLO
- MILD FLAVOR, MEATY TEXTURE

REMOVE GILLS + STEM

4-6 inches

CREMINI
- AKA BABY PORTOBELLOS
- MILD FLAVOR

MAITAKE
AKA
N OF THE WOODS
LICATE, BUT PACKED
W/ FLAVOR
CH + EARTHY

SHIITAKE
- SAVORY + MEATY
- ADDS UMAMI TO DISHES
- POPULAR IN ASIAN COOKING

OYSTER
- CAN BE GRAY, PINK, GREEN OR YELLOW!
- THEY'RE GREAT BATTERED + FRIED
- SLIGHTLY CHEWY

RECIPES TO TRY

DON'T FORGET TO WRITE DOWN WHERE YOU GOT IT!

Grocery list

HONEY

HUMANS HAVE BEEN EATING HONEY FOR AT LEAST 8,000 YRS!

SWEET, VISCOUS FOOD MADE BY BEES FROM FLORAL NECTAR

THE HONEY BEE POLLINATES 3/4 OF THE FRUITS, VEGGIES + NUTS WE EAT IN THE PROCESS OF MAKING HONEY

NICE TONGUE

BEE BARF

BASICALLY, HONEY IS BEE BARF. BEES COLLECT NECTAR + STORE IT IN A SEPARATE STOMACH WHERE IT MIXES W/ ENZYMES, CHANGING THE CHEMICAL COMPOSITION OF IT. IT'S PASSED FROM BEE TO BEE (BY MOUTH) 'TIL IT REACHES THE HONEYCOMB TO BE STORED AS FOOD

"WILDFLOWER" HONEY IS A BLANKET TERM FOR HONEY FROM MANY DIFFERENT FLOWERS. TASTE WILL VARY BASED ON WHERE IT PRODUCED + WHAT FLOWERS ARE IN SEASON

WILDFLOWER
YOU KNOW ME
SUPERMARKET STUFF
• RELIABLE
• FAMILIAR TASTE
• CLEAR
• CHEAP
• ONE-NOTE
• SWEEEEET

EXPERATION
EXP: NEVER

VS

Raw HONEY
NEVER HEATED or FILTERED
• NOT TOO SWEET!
• HIGH LEVELS OF VITAMINS + MINERALS
ORANGE BLOSSOM
THE GOOD STUFF
DELICATE, NUANCED FLAVORS

FLAVOR
IS INFLUENCED BY WHAT **FLOWERS** THE BEES FEED ON

TRUE STORY— HONEY NEVER GOES BAD IN A TIGHTLY SEALED CONTAINER!

QUALITY CHECK

HOW TO SPOT THE GOOD STUFF:
• LISTS THE PLACE IT WAS HARVESTED
ACIDITY + SWEETNESS CAN TASTE HINTS OF WHAT IT'S MADE FROM
CONSISTENCY IS PARTIALLY SOLID OR CONTAINS PART OF THE HONEYCOMB
LOOKS CREAMY
CRYSTALLIZES AT ROOM TEMP

TASTING NOTES
FLORAL, FRUITY, SPICY, SMOKY, EARTHY, WOODY + NUTTY

IN THE SPRING OR SUMMER MONTHS, LOOK FOR HONEY AT YOUR FARMERS' MARKET

SO MANY COLORS!
FACTORS THAT AFFECT COLOR:
• FLOWER SOURCE • HEAT • TIME
COLOR AFFECTS FLAVOR
MILD ⟶ STRONG

GOES GREAT W/ NUTS, APPLES, CHEESE, BREAD, CHOCOLATE + YOGURT. SWEETEN SAUCES, SALAD DRESSINGS, CAKE, COOKIES, PIE + COCKTAILS

RECIPES TO TRY

DON'T FORGET TO WRITE DOWN WHERE YOU GOT IT!

Grocery list

BOBA

NVENTED IN THE 1980s N TAIWAN, THE WORD "BOBA" REFERS TO THICK, BLACK, CHEWY BALLS AT THE BOTTOM OF DRINKS LIKE ICED GREEN TEA, MILK TEA, ICED COFFEE, SLUSHIES + SMOOTHIES. EARLIER VERSIONS USED WHITE, SMALLER "PEARLS"

BOBA GET SUCKED UP THROUGH EXTRA-FAT STRAWS + ARE CHEWED

PIERCE THE FILM W/ THE POINTY END OF THE STRAW

"BOBA TEA" BECAME THE TERMINOLOGY IN CALIFORNIA + "BUBBLE TEA" IN NEW YORK + VANCOUVER

FROM TAIWAN IT SPREAD TO NORTH AMERICA

LATE 1990s
THE 1ST BOBA TEA SHOP OPENED IN LOS ANGELES

ADE OF APIOCA FLOUR, HICH IS FROM HE CASSAVA OOT

ALLS ARE OILED IN 20 THEN DDED TO A WEET SYRUP

IT'S COMMON FOR CUPS TO BE SEALED W/ A THIN, PLASTIC FILM. NOT ONLY IS IT THE TRADITIONAL TAIWANESE STYLE, IT'S CHEAPER FOR THE TEA SHOP. YOU CAN STACK OR SHAKE CUPS EASILY + IT PREVENTS SPILLING

EARLY 2000s
A SLEW OF SHOPS OPENED IN THE SAN GABRIEL VALLEY IN LA, BY IMMIGRANTS OF TAIWANESE DESCENT

1/4"

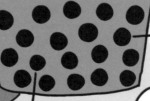

SOFT, CHEWY CONSISTENCY (LIKE GUMMY CANDY)

"BOBA" IS SLANG USED TO DESCRIBE WOMEN W/ BIG BREASTS

RECIPES TO TRY

DON'T FORGET TO WRITE DOWN WHERE YOU GOT IT!

Grocery list

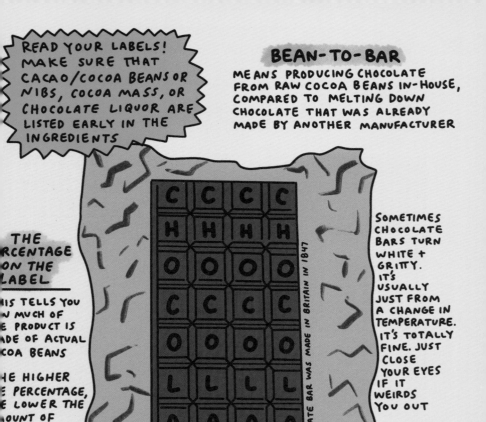

READ YOUR LABELS! MAKE SURE THAT CACAO/COCOA BEANS OR NIBS, COCOA MASS, OR CHOCOLATE LIQUOR ARE LISTED EARLY IN THE INGREDIENTS

BEAN-TO-BAR

MEANS PRODUCING CHOCOLATE FROM RAW COCOA BEANS IN-HOUSE, COMPARED TO MELTING DOWN CHOCOLATE THAT WAS ALREADY MADE BY ANOTHER MANUFACTURER

THE RCENTAGE ON THE LABEL

IS TELLS YOU N MUCH OF E PRODUCT IS DE OF ACTUAL COA BEANS

HE HIGHER E PERCENTAGE, E LOWER THE OUNT OF GAR

THE FIRST CHOCOLATE BAR WAS MADE IN BRITAIN IN 1847

SOMETIMES CHOCOLATE BARS TURN WHITE + GRITTY. IT'S USUALLY JUST FROM A CHANGE IN TEMPERATURE. IT'S TOTALLY FINE. JUST CLOSE YOUR EYES IF IT WEIRDS YOU OUT

CHOCOLATE IS OFTEN PACKAGED IN FOIL BECAUSE IT KEEPS OUT AIR, LIGHT + MOISTURE

UPER DARK HOCOLATE N'T MORE ITTER, IT'S UST LACKING WEETNESS

THE CACAO POD IS SOOOO COOL

HITE CHOCOLATE IS NOT CHOCOLATE! COA SOLIDS ARE WHAT DEFINE CHOCOLATE, VING IT THAT CHOCOLATEY FLAVOR + WHITE HOCOLATE DOESN'T CONTAIN ANY. ONE OF ITS AIN INGREDIENTS IS COCOA BUTTER THOUGH (FROM COA BEANS), SO THEY'RE DEFINITELY RELATED

CHOCOLATE IS MADE FROM A FRUIT + IT'S GROWN IN DIFFERENT PARTS OF THE WORLD, SO IT CAN TASTE VERY DIFFERENT— FROM FRUITY TO FLORAL, EARTHY TO BITTER, SPICY + CREAMY

HUNGRY FOR MORE? CHECK OUT
EAT THIS BOOK!